Open and Innocent

the gentle, passionate art of not-knowing

Scott Morrison

OPEN AND INNOCENT

THE GENTLE, PASSIONATE ART

OF

NOT-KNOWING

Second Edition

by Scott Morrison

American Zen Society Press

Atlanta, Georgia

Second Edition

Copyright © 1992 by J. Scott Morrison

All Rights Reserved

Printed in U. S. A.

ISBN 1-882496-00-0

Library of Congress 92-885577

Zen Buddhism / Meditation / Psychology-Philosophy

American Zen Society Press

315 Breakwater Ridge

Atlanta, GA 30328

(800)745-7814

To You

This book is dedicated to you, the reader. It is best read slowly, with the heart, rather than quickly with the mind. Whether or not you are awake or free, whether you love unconditionally or live wholeheartedly in any given moment, in *this* moment, is *entirely up to you.* Simple, but in most cases, not so easy. What follows are some understandings that have been enormously helpful to me in realizing this truth. No one, myself included, is an authority. I offer them to you as a friend, in the hope that some of them will prove useful.

We all share this human experience; we're in this together and none of us can be excluded. Can we do this openly, honestly and sincerely, without shame or fear? When the secrets all are told, we discover there never was anything that needed to be hidden. Awareness, truth, love and even God (if that term means anything to you) do not depend on anything. May you know the peace that depends on nothing.

Scott Morrison
Asheville, North Carolina, 1992.

Contents

Author's Note

I am not a guru or a religious leader or any sort
of special person. For one thing, I tend to fall off
pedestals too easily. For another, it has become
increasingly apparent to me over the years
that in spite of the fact that we all have a great
deal to teach each other and learn from each
other, none of us is an authority. We may
project that onto certain people, some of whom
are more than happy to play the role, but it is
a simple fact that nobody, no tradition, no
religion, no group or institution, can rescue us
from our lives. Whether we think of ourselves
or others as big people or little people, parents
or children, we each must face the realities of
being human and take responsibility for our
own freedom and happiness. Buddha was just
a person, and virtually everyone I have ever
learned anything useful from did not pretend
to be anybody special. Why should they? Life
itself, and our own True Nature, yours and
mine, is a miracle beyond compare!The infor-
mation in this book is not so much from a
philosophy as from my life, offered with sincerity, affection and compassion.

Everyday pain and discomfort are inevitable -
they go with the nerve endings. Suffering, on
the other hand, is entirely optional and unnec-
essary. I hope this book makes that simple fact
at least a little clearer.

In this book there are several lines of investigation that, if taken personally and deeply enough, with diligence and stubbornness, can radically change the course of your life, as they have countless others before you. Among them are the sections on time, change, peace, making friends with fear, concepts vs. experience, self, being without defense, motive, difficulty, hope and love.

Agreeing or disagreeing with any of this will serve no function. Intellectual understanding changes nothing. To know the truth of anything, you must look personally and deeply and very honestly, without the obstruction of prior opinion, mine, yours or anyone else's. More often than not, it's neither easy nor comfortable, but it's worth it. A thousand times over.

It all depends on just how free and happy you want to be.

GOOD LUCK!

Acknowledgements

With great love and gratitude, I would like to acknowledge at least some of the people whose wisdom and compassion have been so very helpful to me. All have books or tapes that are easily acquired from the American Zen Society in Atlanta (including a recommended reading list), or from your local bookstore.

Thich Nhat Hanh
Toni Packer
Stephen Levine
Jack Kornfield
Joanna Macy
Joseph Goldstein
Charlotte "Joko" Beck
Ken Wilber
Alan Clements
Cheri Huber
Buddhadasa
Ram Das
Chad O'Shea
Achaan Chah
Jiddu Krishnamurti
Alan Watts
Dainin Katagiri
Shuryu Suzuki

I would also like to express special thanks to my dear friend, Frances Milam, whose encouragement, love and support made this book possible.

*"Do everything with a mind
that lets go.
If you let go a little,
you will have a little peace.
If you let go a lot,
you will have a lot of peace.
If you let go completely,
you will know complete peace and
freedom.*

*Your struggles with the world will
have come to an end."*

-Achaan Chah

THE WHOLE TEACHING

The path of awakening and liberation
requires that we ask ourselves just
this one fundamental question:

**"Do I wish to live this moment
with as much attention, care and
affection as possible, or am I going
to do something else?"**

There is no point in judging the
"something else" as either good or bad.
It's just that it's important to know
who's making the decisions.

WHY NOT KNOWING?

You Can't See Anybody If You Know What They Look Like

There are many different states of mind and body, but the one that dominates most of the time is memory. Memory includes not only images, concepts, opinions, judgments, intentions, perceptions, interpretations, fantasies, mental conversations and scenarios, but also feelings and sensations in the body. Something about your appearance or tone of voice may remind me of a particular kind of experience - emotions, feelings and all - that I've had with similar people all my life. That feeling-memory reverberates through my entire body and mind, and if I am unaware of what is happening, I will project that memory experience onto you, therefore keeping myself from any fresh, new, direct contact with you. To whatever degree I think and feel I "know" you, I will not be able to actually see you as you are. The same is true for all people, places, things, activities, and even my own body, heart and mind. If prior "knowledge" or opinion or feeling are the dominant factors and I am unaware of that fact, they will color, distort and oftentimes interfere entirely with direct perception, and I will not be able to discover or experience anything clearly or freely or without conflict.

This is the way it is for most of us most of the time.

HOW IT IS

Take just a moment, if you will, to look at your life as you are living it right now. Be as honest as you can. Are you at peace? Do you love freely and without conditions? This present moment is all that you have. It's all you will ever have. Joy and happiness are here for the taking. All you have to do is surrender - fall openly and unguardedly in love with everyone and everything. Is that possible? What are the options? Just how much attention, understanding, affection and compassion are we capable of, right here, right now? Is there some other time or place that would be better?

REALIZATION
IN EVERYDAY LIFE

You and I have, intrinsically, the capacity to
see and understand ourselves and each other
clearly and wholly from instant to instant; to
see, hear, feel and respond freely without the
distorting, crippling limitations of the self-
centered, soap opera versions of our lives that
dominate our thinking most of the time. We
have, not theoretically but actually, the ability
to be, this very moment, unconditionally liber-
ated and creatively happy, effortlessly func-
tioning with very great love, wisdom and compassion.

Yet we don't seem to live this way. Why is this
so?

That most of us understand the importance of
living with more awareness, love and wisdom
is a given. But the nuts-and-bolts, exactly how
to go about doing that on a real life basis often
seems elusive, if not impossible. If we look
carefully and honestly at the moment-to-mo-
ment reality of how we live our lives, it seems
apparent that we're not there for most of it. We
seem to be oblivious so much of the time to the
people, places, things and activities around us,
almost as if we're half asleep, in a dream state

of worries, regrets, longings, hesitations and distractions. Indeed, it's not unfair to say that most of what we do, we do halfheartedly, as if we don't really want to be there. The numbing effect this has on the quality of our lives is ultimately both undeniable and tragic.

Is it unreasonable to say that when we look at each other, we should actually be able to see each other? And when we listen to each other, we should actually be able to hear one another? And when we pause to take in the silence of a forest in winter, or the wonder in a baby's eyes, or the stunning beauty of a starlit sky, we should actually be able to enjoy those things, too. Otherwise, what's the point in looking or listening or even being alive, if we're not there for it?

Yet the way we live, we rarely seem to be in real touch with much of anything. We walk down the street, covering maybe five or ten blocks, and remember little or nothing of what we saw or heard or even thought. And upon arriving at our destination, we may not even have a clear awareness of how we got there! What's more, we may live with someone for many years, perhaps even someone we say we love, and never actually see that person. That's very serious! (And unfortunately, very, very common.) What's worse still, is that when we are not in contact with each other, with our surroundings, who else are we not in contact with?

We are completely out of touch with ourselves: our own bodies, hearts and minds.

This small tragedy is lived out, it seems, most days of our lives, and the simple fact of the matter is that it doesn't have to be that way. Because even though they are somewhat rare, we do have moments of close and deep contact with ourselves and each other, and the fact that they occur at all suggests that it may be possible to live more this way. Indeed, that very possibility is the central focus of a great deal of consciousness research, transpersonal and spectrum psychology, deep ecology and general systems theory, as well as the mystical (albeit somewhat mystified) traditions of Buddhism, Taoism, Sufism, Christianity, Vedanta Hinduism, Judaism, native Shamanism and others. What these various disciplines are working towards, however disputatiously on the surface, is the human process of realization, enlightenment and liberation. And in personal, down-to-earth terms, the wonderful secret of realization is that when we are in full contact with our bodies, hearts and minds, we are also in full contact with our environment, our activities and each other. Realization does not, indeed cannot, exclude anything or anybody!

So again, how is this accomplished in day-to-day, real life terms? Although not necessarily so easy, the process is really quite simple, almost startlingly so. In any given moment, if we are willing to let go of our expectations and demands of how things are "supposed to be" and surrender our full attention and care to how they actually are, realization occurs on its own. It comes as a gift, undemanded and uninvited, when the mind is still and open, not in want or fear, not in pursuit of anything. It occurs not because we will it or make it happen - we don't have that capacity - but because we allow it to happen. It's very important to understand that it requires no discipline or control on our part, but rather a deep and passionate curiosity and sensitivity to what is here in this moment - whatever person, place, activity lies in the path of our awareness, right here, right now. To experience it, you don't even have to lift your eyes from this page. Only to surrender yourself to uncompromising attention, love and care for whatever is present.

WILLINGNESS & OPENNESS
ARE THE KEYS

If you think back over the happiest times of your life, you will find central to each one of those moments a quality of love and surrender, the giving of yourself over to the experience at hand. It may have been that you allowed it to happen quite naturally, even unconsciously. You may have discovered yourself falling in love with a place, watching the sunset on the edge of a cliff at Big Sur or the Grand Canyon or some quiet wood near your home. It may have been a moment of intense affection or compassion for someone close to you, a child or a friend or a lover or someone in your family. You may have given yourself over to some activity, the creation of something, a song or a sculpture or a part in a play, perhaps even something normally considered commonplace, yet very personal and special to you in that moment.

So why can't we just live like that? If joy, happiness and peace are so accessible, why not just be that way? Yes, why not? Have you tried it? What happens?

Even if we understand the gravity of the situation, even if we wholeheartedly commit ourselves to the present moment, how long does it last? Even if I say I want to, that I'm going to live each moment of my life with as much awareness, love and care as possible from here on out, "ready... set... go!," what do I find myself doing 45 minutes later? Perhaps 45 seconds?

The fact is that even though it's amazingly simple, it's also amazingly difficult. Because we forget. We have spent an entire lifetime being trained and continuing to train ourselves that happiness is found anywhere but this present moment. So no matter how determined or strong-willed we may be, we get lost at the drop of a hat. Over and over and over again. Sometimes it seems hopeless.

But is it? Not if we realize the gravity of the situation. Not if we realize that it's our happiness (as well as, to a considerable degree, the happiness of those around us) that's at stake. Not if we realize that what's in question is our capacity to actually live our lives intimately, caringly, creatively and wholeheartedly.

If, in the face of the enormity of the task, we are willing to work diligently, sometimes stubbornly, to discover deeply and personally how thoroughly our own psycho-physiological conditioning colors, distorts, interferes and controls everything we do, keeping us divided and in conflict with each other, our environment and even within ourselves, and to discover the glue that holds this all together, then a great deal may be possible. With that stopping, looking and investigating directly, we may find that the structure begins to slip. Its credibility begins to fade because the only thing that keeps us in bondage and confusion is ignorance, lack of clear understanding. And even the slightest taste of freedom cannot be denied.

To begin, it is pointless to think of liberation as some kind of future goal. Rather, it must be seen as the fundamental first step. Without it, there can be no love and no happiness. There must first be the freedom to investigate carefully without knowing in advance, from prior opinion or expectation, how it's going to come out. Then, and only then can we discover what's true.

MISUNDERSTANDING TIME

There Is No Day After Tomorrow

Consider the question of time. Most of us suffer from a misunderstanding, and a gross one at that, of what time is. To explain, practically all of us subscribe to the continuum view of time. That is, my life, if represented on this page, might look something like this:

Birth_____me now(.)__ old age____death.

This convention may be useful as a way of organizing, keeping track of and comparing my various memories, but it doesn't really give me a true picture of my life. There is no real line running through the room you're sitting in right now. There never has been. It's only a thought form, a way of representing our lives, not the real thing. We can't feel it, touch it, taste it, hear it, see it or otherwise experience it outside of the mind because it's imaginary, a mental construct.

Yet when you ask most people what past, present and future are to them, they will pro-ceed to tell you about an enormous area of their experience that includes thousands of things that have happened to them, terrible and won-derful and mundane and shocking and silly and so on. This they call "the past". They will then tell about an even larger area of experi-ences that may happen, terrible and wonderful and funny and unforeseen and so forth, and this they refer to as "the future". If they refer to a present at all, it is only a tiny, tiny point, barely noticed in passing, as they ricochet back and forth from past to future to past to future. This is very telling, because it reveals how very much we seem to be fixated, viewing our lives primarily through a very dominant filter of obsessive thinking about situations that do not exist outside of the mind.

All of this, fortunately, is based on a hallucination. For if we look at it very carefully and honestly, we will notice that *there is no such thing as "the past", there is only present memory* - that is, present traces in our brain cells and body tissues of people, places, things, activities, conversations and events, along with our perceptions and interpretations and emotional and physical reactions to them. *All of this occurs entirely in the present.* (Not the concept, "present time", but here, now. There is no other "time" for it to occur.) Indeed, present memory is the only way I can have a clear sense that there were presents before this one. But with a little further examination, it becomes clear that there never has been, or ever will be, any "time" other that this present, meaning that there is *no such thing as a real, actual past that is somehow separate and distinct from the present.* All of what we call the past is only memory, a very small part of present experience. For instance, I had a close friend named Tom who died unexpectedly of a massive heart attack a few years ago. There's no way I can go back into a real time called the past and tell him how much I appreciated his friendship.

It's too late - it's over and done with. What I have now are present memories of things we did and said and my interpretations of them and so forth. Some bring me sorrow and some make me smile, but they are all in the present.

In like terms, *everything we call "the future" is nothing but memory rearranged so that it looks like it will occur day after tomorrow or next month and projected holographically as fantasy,* based primarily on what we like and dislike (at the time), what we remember gave us pleasure or pain, comfort or discomfort, what we have the strongest emotional and neuromuscular and endocrine responses to. Because these present rearrangements of memory, present anticipations, have such a high likelihood of coming true, and on top of that, because we have such a strong tendency to see what we expect to see (perception shaped by memory) and even influence reality by what we expect to see (self-fulfilling prophesy), we come to believe that this present expectation is a real, actual future that is, again, separate from the present. But, of course, once more we discover that we can't go into this future to find out what is going to happen next year and then come back here and impress our friends. Because it doesn't exist. It's imaginary.

Well, so what? Even if it is the case that we've unconsciously created some kind of hypnotic state with these notions of past, present and future that aren't really accurate, what's the harm in it? It seems like the natural way to look at it - certainly it's the way practically everybody else looks at it. What's the problem?

The problem is that even if we intellectually understand that time is fictitious, that this present is all that we ever have, have had or will have, we don't seem to get any points for that level of understanding. For if we proceed to live, as we have since early childhood, as if the past and future are not only separate, actual times, but somehow, more important than the present, then we deprive ourselves of awareness of the only moment we can ever enjoy anything, the only time we can ever truly know peace, joy, love, freedom, happiness, wisdom, compassion - the very things we say our lives are about!

Furthermore, when we spend our time regretting or longing for the the past, or worrying about or longing for something in the future, we find we have created problems that have no solutions. Because they are based on remembered or imagined situations, we have no way of doing anything about them. If, however, I realize that the problem is not with the hurts I suffered in childhood (those are over), but rather with my present experience of (and fear of facing) those unresolved and very real present memories of pain, embarrassment, humiliation or terror stored in my mind and body now, then I suddenly realize I have a clear choice as to whether I will assume responsibility for my own healing or not.

In regard to future concerns, if I realize that the process of worrying about not being able to pay my bills next month or losing my relationship or not getting something I regard as important (those things haven't happened yet) is basically a waste of energy, then I am freed up to enjoy and do and be whatever is here and necessary right now. Not only can I let go of the tension and conflict of future demand and expectation and fear, but I find I can actually live my life rather than just thinking or worrying about it. And, as a bonus, the future, because it flows out of the present, takes care of itself.

All of this sounds very simple, and it is. But it's also important to realize that this doesn't necessarily make life that much easier, just more workable. And it returns responsibility and freedom back where they belong (where they have been all along): in my own lap, right here, right now.

HOW IT WORKS

We each have to attend to our own awakening
and liberation, but the task is often much
easier and sometimes more enjoyable by sup-
porting and being supported by friends who are
committed to doing the same. The simple practice of mindfulness (insight meditation) and
meditative inquiry is perhaps the clearest and
most direct way of freeing ourselves. It is ex-
tremely practical and effective, and not difficult to understand. It is taught all over the
country, in schools, churches, hospitals, hos-
pices, 12-step groups, bookstores, adult educa-
tion centers, universities, monasteries and re-
treat centers. The following is a basic introduc-
tion.

Several prior considerations will be helpful:

OPENNESS, HONESTY & SINCERITY

The first has to do with openness, honesty and sincerity. It is perhaps obvious by now that this kind of endeavor requires an enormous amount of sincerity and willingness to honestly investigate the direct, unembellished truth of your life in this present moment. In most cases, this is not easy, for the first things we see when we actually look directly for the first time are boredom, restlessness, craving, conflict, tension, resistance, sorrow, guilt, worry, anger, disappointment, frustration and *in*-sincerity. In other words, a mind that is totally out of control. So it will require not only an honesty about what you discover, but a willingness to be as compassionate and forgiving with yourself as possible. In fairness, we didn't consciously sign up to be the way we are, and it's exceedingly wise to be as gentle (and non-judgemental) with ourselves as possible.

THE HALF-SMILE

The second is something called the Half-Smile of the Buddha, a gentle acknowledgement that you actually care enough about yourself and your life to be doing this, if for no other reason, simply because it feels good, even when you find yourself facing fear, anger or sorrow. Often it's a kind of *chutzpah* in the face of difficulty. In the practice of yoga, one assumes a certain posture and shortly begins to feel much better. Vietnamese Zen master Thich Nhat Hanh calls the half-smile "mouth yoga".

POSTURE

The third is posture. Sitting in your normal way, think of something depressing. Now sitting up straight, comfortable and relaxed, but not leaning on anything, with head, neck and spine aligned, think of the same thing. Does it affect you the same way? Somehow sitting up straight offers a kind of clarity and energy that slouching doesn't (maybe our mothers were right). In any case, students and teachers of hatha yoga discovered this thousands of years ago, and it's their business to know, since it was developed as an aid to people who were sitting in meditation 16 hours a day. Does that mean we can't be aware slouching or lying down or walking rapidly to work? Of course not, but since we need all the help we can get, it's worth a try.

STILLNESS

The fourth is stillness. In spite of the fact that books on meditation often make it sound like all you have to do is quiet your mind, in reality it doesn't turn out to be so easy (you may have already discovered that). However, even if we can't so readily still our minds, we can still our bodies, and interestingly, after having done that for even just a few moments, our minds tend to follow suit. A peace and joy and a spaciousness which makes clear observation much easier begins to set in.

LIGHTHEARTEDNESS

Finally, there is rapture (lightheartedness, playfulness, controlled folly), one of the seven factors of enlightenment. You will be seeing a lot of things about yourself that do not necessarily fit in very well with your old self images and self concepts, perhaps some of them shocking. You will begin to get street-wise with your mind, and, seeing its motives, be less likely to believe its latest opinions and story lines. In this it is very useful to have a sense of humor, a playfulness, an amused skepticism, even irreverence toward formerly and sometimes rigidly held absolutes.

THE DEEPER LEVELS OF

HAPPINESS

Most of us have a very narrow view of happiness, having been conditioned to think of it in connection with only a small number of experiences. There are, in fact, many different levels of happiness, and the level of sense pleasure is the lowest on the scale. This includes enjoying beautiful sights and sounds, smells and tastes, wonderful feelings in the body, even certain mental pleasures. Unfortunately, very few of us even get much more than the briefest taste of this basic level of enjoyment. The cause (as in cause and effect), that is, the condition which allows it to happen, is **purity of intention**. It is a direct result of love, generosity and not causing harm to ourselves and others. Since so much of our attention is taken up by the process of greed and anger (to say nothing of denial and escape), we have little energy left to enjoy even the most basic of life's pleasures. America, famous for its obsession with sex, is more obsessed with the *idea of sex* than the reality, with very few people free and present enough to enjoy it. The same is true for all other sense pleasures. Experiment with intention yourself and watch what happens.

ABSORPTION

Beyond the sense pleasurses and the heaven realms are the various levels of bliss that come as a result of **purity of mind**, concentration and absorption. All of these levels can be reached by developing mindfulness of breathing.

LIBERATION

The highest levels of happiness, however, come as a result of **purity of view**, the coming into balance and maturity of concentration, mindfulness and wisdom, and they include all of the lower levels. Cultivating this level is the primary focus of this book.

It is pointless to speculate what these various levels might be like, however, because all we are doing is creating, out of memory, a fantasy rather than a reality. Obviously the only course of action is to look and see. Real skills are required (concentration and mindful inquiry), and the only way we will actually know is to develop them and find out for ourselves.

YOGIC BREATHING

To begin developing absorption, try this:

Breathing diaphragmatically (into the belly), inhale to a count of 4 and exhale to a count of 4, with no pause between breaths. Divide your attention evenly between the counting and the sensation of breathing. As your concentration gets stronger and your attention gets continuous and precise, drop the counting. If it gets scattered, return to the counting until it gets strong again. Watch what happens when you maintain strong concentration for even just a few moments.

As you begin to experience the deeper levels of joy, tranquility and stength of mind associated with absorption, you may find you want to practice for 10 or 20 minutes prior to mindfulness practice for the pure pleasure of it.

And that's nothing. Watch what happens when you apply that increased concentration to mindful investigation. You will discover a richness of texture in each new object that you will not be able to put into words.

DISCOVERING
"THE MIRACLE OF MINDFULNESS"

The basic practice begins with mindfulness of breath. Thirty minutes to an hour, twice a day, if possible. (Five minutes, once a day is infinitely better than nothing!) If you miss a day, no guilt or blame, just get back on track the next day.

Getting comfortable and relaxed, letting the belly be soft, the jaw and mouth relax, the eyes be soft, simply let the breath breathe itself, with your full attention on the sensations of breathing in the abdominal region. Nothing to control. Just let yourself enjoy this breath. No discipline necessary. Just gentle curiosity about this breath. This present one. Let this quiet awareness of breathing be the anchor for your attention. (As you develop skill in being with it, you will also begin to notice it outside of formal practice at various times of the day and evening and in various situations. It will thus begin to serve as an reminder to be here now, an awakening bell.)

Deepening attention on this present breath

allows a healing peace to sink in.

It is only a small step from mindfulness of breath to mindfulness of the whole body, to mindfulness of feelings (based in the body, based in the mind), then to mindfulness of mental formations, perceptions, intentions, thoughts and emotional reactions, and finally mindfulness of consciousness and its objects (seeing, hearing, smelling, tasting, feeling and thinking). In other words, once you have arrived, that is, once you have become aware of your breath and your body, and become established in that awareness, you can open it up to everything.

Let awareness of an object come to you. Let it become you. Let yourself become it. Thought, feeling, sound, whatever. No effort. Just gentle, open awareness. Whatever becomes predominant, let that be the object of your investigation, not in an analytical way, but in a direct, experiential way. If nothing else is calling your attention, return to the breath.

It's important to remember that mindfulness and concentration are skills, perhaps the most important we can develop. Therefore, if they appear weak or scattered, especially in the beginning, keep in mind that, like all skills, they can and will be developed with diligence and gentle perseverance. Precision and continuity are most important in the beginning. Your attention may wander continuously and you may have to bring yourself back hundreds of times, but eventually you will get it. One of my earlier teachers, Jack Kornfield, a Buddhist monk who became a psychologist and taught from that combined perspective, had a great metaphor, "Training the mind is like training a puppy," he said, "you put him down and tell him to 'stay'. Does he stay? Of course not. He jumps on you or runs into the next room. Again, you set him down. 'Stay.' Again, he's off. Over and over. Perhaps sixty-five times. You gently persist. Suddenly, on the sixty-sixth, he stays! He's begun to get the point, at least for the time being." Gentle persistence. Precision and continuity.

As these skills do develop, many things become apparent that were previously hidden: how memory of pleasurable and painful events, likes and dislikes, unexperienced and unhealed events colors and distorts how we see the world, ourselves and each other, how motive (love, greed, generosity, anger, understanding, ignorance) determines the quality of each moment as well as future ones, what the characteristics of life are, how love works.

Intellectual understanding of these things has no effect. There are no fundamental changes. We have to investigate them personally, directly, experientially. The understanding that arises from these direct insights offers us much clearer choices and a great deal more freedom from fear, frustration, disappointment, sorrow and loneliness.

As you notice there is no permanent, solid, stable you, you begin to see that you are your experience. Everything in your life is a flow of phenomena, and you begin to see that you are that flow. The feeling of isolation, separation and loneliness begins to fall away. Fear, anger and sorrow begin to fade. The seeing, hearing and feeling directly is the letting go! This is not an easy path, but one of great joy and beauty, sensitivity, freedom and love. I wish you well on your journey.

HOW TO GET HERE

The following are some devices, some ancient and some modern, that I have found useful in bringing my attention home. You can use the words if it helps, but the awareness is what is important.

**BREATHING IN,
I KNOW THAT I AM BREATHING IN
BREATHING OUT,
I KNOW THAT I AM BREATHING OUT**

**I AM BREATHING IN A LONG (OR SHORT) BREATH
I AM BREATHING OUT A LONG (OR SHORT) BREATH**

**BREATHING IN,
I AM AWARE OF MY WHOLE BODY
BREATHING OUT,
I AM AWARE OF MY WHOLE BODY**

**BREATHING IN,
I CALM THE ACTIVITIES OF MY BODY
BREATHING OUT,
I CALM THE ACTIVITIES OF MY BODY**

BREATHING IN, I CALM MY BODY
BREATHING OUT, I SMILE
DWELLING IN THE PRESENT MOMENT
I KNOW THIS
IS A WONDERFUL MOMENT
(From Thich Nhat Hanh)

I AM AWARE OF THE POSITION OF MY
BODY
(sitting, standing, walking, lying)

I AM AWARE OF MY BODILY ACTIONS
(moving, speaking, dressing, eating, drink-
ing, going to the bathroom, driving, writing, talking on the telephone, resting, falling asleep, waking up)

I AM AWARE OF MY BODY
(from bottom to top, from top to bottom,
body part-by-body part)

I AM AWARE OF THE INTERDEPEN-
DENCE OF MY BODY AND THE UNI-
VERSE
(matter, solid, hard, liquid, permeating,
warm, cool, movement)

I AM AWARE THAT
MY BODY IS CHANGING
(contemplation on the body from before
conception, as genetic elements in your
parents' bodies, your grandparents' bodies and so on, contemplation on yourself
as a fetus growing in your mother's womb,
your body as a baby, a child, an adoles-
cent, an adult, an elderly person, contemplating your body dying, decomposing, be-
coming parts of other beings)

I AM AWARE THAT MY BODY IS MADE
UP ENTIRELY OF A FLOW OF ELE-
MENTS FROM OUTSIDE OF ITSELF
(contemplating interdependence: how we
are made up of water, groundwater,
clouds, animals, plants, minerals from the
soil, photosynthesis, sunshine, oxygen,
carbon dioxide, as well as the work of the
farmer, the truck driver, the grocer, their
families, parents, grandparents and so
on)

I AM AWARE OF A PLEASANT (UNPLEAS-
ANT, NEUTRAL) FEELING
(noticing whether it is based in the body
or the mind, and the interplay between
the two)

I AM AWARE OF LONGING (DISLIKING,
RESISTING, AVOIDING) IN MY MIND

I AM AWARE OF AN INTENTION
(to crave, to cling, to love, to share, to give, to hate, to harm, to avoid, to escape, to attack, to understand, to observe)

I AM AWARE OF A MENTAL FUNCTION
(thoughts, mental images, scenarios, conversations, memory, fantasy, perception, interpretation)

**I AM AWARE OF A
PHENOMENON FADING**
(the dissolution of a bodily sensation, a feeling, an intention, a perception, a mental formation or emotional state)

**I AM AWARE OF CONSCIOUSNESS
AND ITS OBJECT**
(seeing, hearing, smelling, tasting, feeling, thinking)

Investigation,
Love & Liberation

The following section is composed of considerations, which if investigated thoroughly, will result in much joy, happiness, peace and freedom from suffering. Just how much will depend entirely on the quality of your own willingness, openness and honesty. Please do not take my word for any of these things. Do not take anyone else's word. Do not settle for your own prior opinions on these things. Rather, look and see for yourself. May you discover freedom!

FLOWERS IN AIR

This is not to say that memory and fantasy, as well as technical and rational thinking, have no useful function. Of course they do. Planning ahead (skillfully using the creative memory-fantasy capabilities of the brain) and learning from memory so as not to repeat our mistakes are wise present uses of those capacities. Our problem is that, as a rule, we do not think rationally or wisely, but mechanically and blindly, without examining or questioning the process at all. Why trust memory and fantasy as if they were the ultimate authority? For the most part, they function like a cross between a soap opera and a beer commercial. We automatically believe them and they're not even real. What's more, they're hurtful. No human being is going to go to the trouble of insulting you hundreds of times a week. Memory and fantasy will.

THE PEACE THAT DEPENDS ON NOTHING

We cannot create peace. Peace is what happens when we stop

                  clinging
                  craving
                  hoping
                  expecting
                  demanding
                  judging
                  denying
                  resisting
                  attacking
                  condemning
                  blaming
                  hating
                  worrying
                  fearing
                  dividing
                  separating
                  competing
                  lying
               hurting others
               hurting yourself

and holding onto how we want things to be.

Without those kinds of intentions, we are free to start doing things out of awareness and caring and compassion and sharing and love for the person(s), place, thing, or activity at hand.

That's peace.

When You've Made Friends with

Fear, Who Can Frighten You?

When You've Made Friends with

Sorrow, Who Can Hurt You?

Get to know your fear and sorrow well, including the thoughts, memories, fantasies, feelings and sensations in the body that arise when you are in those states. It may not feel good and it seems very difficult the first time or two, but if you are courageous and persevering in your effort, you will notice that it gets a little easier each time. Emboldened by your success, persist until you no longer need to fear them. Learn to welcome them and be at ease with them.

"Well, hello, fear. Hello, terror! Oh, and there's embarrassment and shame right behind you. Please sit down and have a cup of tea!"

They will not stay long. With no resistance, they will return less frequently and tend to fade much quicker.

LOVE IS FREEDOM

Love is by its own nature unconditional. It has no possessions or attachments. It is not in pursuit of anything, and therefore does not fear anything. It has no dependencies. It does not cling to anything, and is therefore without frustration, envy, anger, jealosy, disappointment or sorrow. It is freedom.

Our problems are not with love, but the things call love, which are really craving, clinging, depending, projecting, manipulating and trying to control. These bring endless misery. They are the process by which we torture ourselves unknowingly, out of ignorance.

Loving has nothing to do with these things. It is beauty and joy beyond measure.

LIFE WITHOUT HOPE

Hope is the great destoyer of life. We secretly think it will bring us happiness and security, but in fact it brings us frustation and disappointment. We hope for relationship, for sex, for money, for success, for recognition, for possessions, for love, for enlightenment, for fame, for stability, for power, for liberation. Does this work? Has it ever? Given that, is it likely to?

It is a simple fact that we cannot enjoy any of the above or anything else in life until we completely give up the process of hoping and start paying attention to what is happening now.

You cannot enjoy making love if you are caught up in hoping to enjoy making love. If you give up that hope, and let yourself be aware and sensitive, then something entirely new and not born of hope or of the thinking process is free to take place. That something that has no name, and has never happened before, nor will it ever happen again. It is wonder and beauty and sweetness itself. That is life without hope. That is freedom.

YOU ARE THE WORLD:

Concepts vs. Experience

There is no Texas

Texas takes up a lot of space on the map, but when you're flying over it on your way across the country, it's a startling discovery! It's not really there! When you look down to find Texas, all you see is desert and rolling hills and a crazy-quilt patchwork of farms and an occasional tiny, silver-blue ribbon meandering through the middle of it all. But no Texas!

Now, I'm not going to be the one to break it to the people who live there, but Texas is nothing more than a concept, an identity, a pattern of images and feelings in the body. Since nobody questions the "reality" of that concept, through sort of a mass hypnosis it takes on the appearance of a substance and a permanence that it doesn't really have. Indeed, when a "Texan" has thoughts about Texas, that person's body reacts with feelings, making "Texas" feel all the more real. Because so many people believe in Texas, we are afraid to question it, for fear of looking like a fool. But look, see for yourself! There is also no Oklahoma, no Pennsylvania, no United States. No Harvard, no government, no Roman Catholic Church. Just people going to work in brick buildings and cathedrals. Just like you and me.

Of course, to some degree it may be wise to go along with the pretense so as not to rile the natives. It serves no function to upset the people who work for the IRS or the Republican Party or *The New York Times* or the Southern Baptist Convention whose livelihoods depend on people believing in those things. But the point is that you and I don't have to deceive ourselves about those "institutions" having any real substantiality or consciousness or power of their own, because they are not real entities.

There is no Scott Morrison

You and I are not different from Texas. When you start looking for your "self", all you find is a constant flow of thoughts and images and opinions and ideas and roles, all made up entirely of memories, accompanied by a flow of bodily sensations, giving us concrete referents, but no permanent, solid, separate, stable "you" to be found anywhere.

And discovering that you are nobody, you also discover that you are everything. You can, in any given moment, distinguish between your head and your foot and your house and your neighbor and your car and the earth and the sky and the forest, but close investigation reveals that those are all a part of you. In other words, there is no part of you that is separate from any other part. Different, yes, but not separate. Every living cell in your body is made up entirely of things you normally think of as "outside of yourself": water, food, plants, animals, minerals from the soil, sunshine, clouds, ground water, an ovum from your mother, a sperm from your father, molecular structures from your parents' bodies, and from their parents' bodies and so on and on. In other words, everything is related and constantly interacting with everything else. Physics tells us this. Biology and ecological sciences tell us this. Psychology tells us this, but far and away the most important, direct observation will reveal beyond a shadow of a doubt, that nothing is or can be separate from anything else. Including us.

The beauty of that very radical realization is that, once we actually see it, feel it, discover it for ourselves, we can stop pretending we are somehow an isolated, lonely, fragile little ego suspended in a solitary confinement with its own problems and longings and fears and regrets and frustrations and worries and disappointments.

You are the world! Are you big enough to embrace it?

"I seem to be a verb."

-Buckminister Fuller

Everything Changes,

EVERYTHING!

Not only is everything constantly inter-acting with everything else, but none of it stays the same from one moment to the next. This is absolutely trustworthy. It's how it all works.

No matter how hard you try, you will not be able to find any experience you can hold onto. You may *think* you can, but investigate directly, see if that is really so. It's not so much a matter of whether you should or shouldn't hold onto anything - it's that you can't - because nothing is stable. And if you make the mistake of telling yourself that something major in your life is not going to change, like your relationship or your job or your success or your fame or your prestige or your political power, the odds of you suffering severe worry, frustration and disappointment are very high. Even simple pleasures and happiness are transient.

The miracle of this realization is that once you see it fully and surrender to the irresistible fact of constant change, it's a relief! There's a taste of freedom as you discover that your unhappiness came, not from impermanence, but from *resisting it!* Take a while and let that one really sink in.

The Process of

Heaven and Hell

The Law of Motive, as plainly as I can put it, is that *the intention or motive behind everything you think, say or do determines the outcome.* That is, it determines the quality of the immediate as well as future experiences, and it establishes the conditions for the arising of that motive again later. It's simple cause and effect. Heaven and hell and everything in between are not determined by the contents, the details, the "what's" of our lives, but rather by the process, the intention, the volition, the "how".

The Contents of Life

The contents are relationships, money, possessions, friends, lovers, jobs, success, failure, health, sickness, hopes, dreams, opinions, children, death, change, sex, recognition, fame, power, infamy, accidents, honors and so on.

The Process of Life

The process, the "how" has to do with attention, understanding, love, generosity, compassion, fearlessness, greed, anger, delusion, denial, fear, resistance, cruelty, avoidance, clinging.

It's not what you do, it's how you do it (with greed or generosity?)
It's not what you say, it's how you say it (with love or denial or envy?)
It's not what you think, it's how you think it (with wisdom or fear?)
It's not what happens to you, but how you are with what happens to you (with awareness or competitiveness or understanding or anger?)

When the dominant motive is love, generosity or wisdom, the result is joy, happiness and beauty.

When the dominant motive is greed, clinging, anger, delusion or denial, the result is ugliness and suffering.

These are general rules, but tend to be amazingly accurate. The primary idea is that if your predominant intention is to **not cause harm,** you will experience happiness as a result. If you think this is some kind of moral or legalistic system that you're *supposed* to live by, *you've totally missed the point!*

In order to find out whether they are true or not, you cannot just agree or disagree. You must experiment with them personally and verify them in your own life. Half measures will not work! In other words, you must be completely open and honest in your experimentation.

For example, if we try to manipulate or control the behavior of our lover and call that "love" we will discover nothing but the frustrating results of our own clinging and dishonesty.

In ancient times, it was

"chop wood, carry water."

Now, it is according to Charlotte "Joko" Beck, an extraordinary Zen teacher in San Diego,

"make love, drive freeway."

The contents have changed, as they always will. The motives and their results are still up to us.

INNOCENCE

BEING WITHOUT DEFENSE

AND

FREEDOM FROM FEAR

Can you be eaten by a tiger and survive it?

Intelligent protection of our bodies and each other is one thing. Psychological defense is entirely another. We assume the latter is necessary because it was learned from parents, peers and other authority figures such a long time ago that it is automatically trusted without questioning it . But does it really work? I get hurt, and immediately my mind begins to replay what happened, why it happened, and what could or should have happened instead. From there it unconsciously, mechnically decides who is to be blamed, myself or somebody else, and proceeds to judge, condemn, gossip, attack, lash out and hate whoever that is. Of course it doesn't actually protect me from my hurt, which I am trying to avoid, so I still must numb it, stuff it or wallow in it. And it just continues to get worse. Furthermore, I isolate myself in "defense" and cut off any possibility of being in open, intimate, vulnerable touch with anybody or anything. Is there any other way?

How about just feeling it? That is, seeing and hearing it, feeling the sensations in my body as they occur, all without trying to escape, attack or defend. It may be very hard, but can I do it anyway?

What do I discover? What was being attacked and run away from and defended against was nothing but a memory! The "little me," the sense of "me" is nothing but memory. It's not really me. And the whole things collapses. Because even though it looked like me and felt like me, it wasn't really made of anything.

Our continuous problem is that we sincerely believe that little sense of self in the memory (or fantasy) is us, and we've never questioned it . We give everything for it, and we will, in some cases, even die for it, and it 's not even real.

Close your eyes. Imagine yourself being attacked by a tiger or some other giant animal that eats people. It will probably feel uncomfortable, but do it anyway. Have it rip your arms and legs off. Bite off your head. *Crunch, crunch.* It's big enough and hungry enough to swallow the whole rest of your body. *Gulp!* Imagine a satisfied look on its face some hours later after it has finished digesting you. Now, open your eyes. Are you still there?

That wasn't you! It is composed entirely of memories, and all of its problems, its hopes, its longings, its tragedies, its fears, its "difficulties with other people", its wants, its likes and dislikes, its "relationships," its possessions, its losses and its sorrows are all ficticious.

The brain simply does not tend to distingish between its own memory-fantasy-feeling process and a real threat to the organism. It's not real and it's not you. And neither are any of its problems. All that leaves you with to attend to and love is the entire rest of the universe and everything that's in it.

**Why trust memory or fantasy?
For the most part they function
like a cross between a soap opera
and a beer commercial.**

As a Rule, Life Is Not Easy.
So What?

As psychiatrist Scott Peck pointed out in the first chapter of *The Road Less Traveled,* paraphrasing Buddha, "life is difficult." He went on to say that this is one of the world's great truths, because once this simple fact is seen and fully accepted, it's not really difficult anymore. In other words, the difficulty no longer matters because it is not being resisted.

This is also true of running, dancing, mountain climbing, writing a book, playing tennis, acting in a play and making love. There are aches and pains and moments of insecurity and awkwardness, maybe even dangers. These do not seem to stop us. Nor should they. We just get on with it because we are given over to the thing itself. If you are totally given over to life itself, bumps and bruises and difficulties and all, then attention and love become the dominant experience.

JUST BE IT!

On Believing In Mind

by Seng-Ts'an

The Great Way is not difficult
For those who have no preferences.
When clinging and resisting are both absent,
Everything is clear and undisguised.
Make the smallest distinction, however,
And heaven and earth
are set infinitely apart.

If you wish to see the truth,
Then hold no opinions for
or against anything.
To set up what you like
against what you dislike -
This is the disease of the mind.

When the deep meaning of things
is not understood
The mind's essential peace
is disturbed to no purpose.

The Way is perfect like unto vast space,
With nothing lacking, nothing in excess:
It is indeed in our choosing to accept or reject
That we do not see the true nature of things.

Pursue not the outer entanglements,
Dwell not in the inner void;
Be serene in the oneness of things
And erroneous views vanish by themselves.

The more you talk and think about it,
The further you wander from the truth.
Therefore, stop talking and thinking,
And there is nothing you will not be able to know.

Do not search for the truth,
Only cease to cherish opinions.
If there is even a trace of this and that, right or wrong,
The mind's essence will be lost in confusion.
Let go, and things follow their own courses,
Obey the nature of things,
And you are in concord with the Way.

The essence of it is to
let yourself see how much
clinging to how you want your life to be
is nothing more
than the process of self-torture,
drop it,
and allow yourself to fall openly and
unguardedly in love with your life
as it is, and everthing in it.

(Continued on page 1.)

If you are interested in receiving notice of future publications, intensives or retreats with Scott Morrison, please contact the

AMERICAN ZEN SOCIETY
315 Breakwater Ridge
Atlanta, GA 30328
(800)745-7814